THE LITTLE BOOK OF
SPELLS

THE LITTLE BOOK OF SPELLS

Copyright © Summersdale Publishers Ltd, 2019

Text by Anna Martin

An Hachette UK Company
www.hachette.co.uk

Summersdale Publishers Ltd
Part of Octopus Publishing Group Limited
Carmelite House
50 Victoria Embankment
LONDON
EC4Y 0DZ
UK

www.summersdale.com

Printed and bound in Poland

ISBN: 978-1-78685-799-6

Substantial discounts on bulk quantities of Summersdale books are available to corporations, professional associations and other organisations. For details contact general enquiries: telephone: +44 (0) 1243 771107 or email: enquiries@summersdale.com.

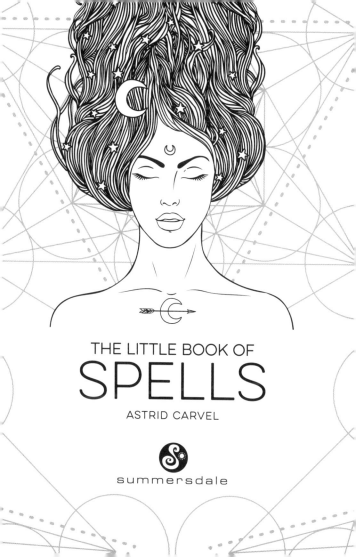

THE LITTLE BOOK OF
SPELLS

ASTRID CARVEL

summersdale

CONTENTS

INTRODUCTION

This little book invites you in to the world of white witchcraft. Perhaps you have always had an affinity for the spiritual realm – you may have a heightened intuition, or maybe you have seen vlogs, blogs or newspaper articles about witchcraft and want to know what all the fuss is about.

Magical energies permeate everything in nature, including ourselves. White witchcraft offers the chance to connect with our inner power and invoke these natural energies for magical purposes. It is also a platform for healing and self-care, reflection, self-expression and self-discovery.

Within these pages you will find a blend of white witchcraft and self-care, which is accessible to everyone, with many of the spells requiring little or no tools to perform them, and all being completely safe. Many also use found natural objects, which can increase a spell's potency – windfall twigs can be fashioned into wands, or you can draw on the power of crystals, herbs and the moon's phases.

The spells in this book are divided into the four elements: earth, air, fire and water. By harnessing the power of the elements and the natural world you will soon discover the magic within you.

WHITE WITCHCRAFT IN THE TWENTY-FIRST CENTURY

For a long period of history, witchcraft was traditionally the realm of those marginalized by society - groups who had a growing sense of disillusionment and lack of personal power turned to ways they could actively improve upon their lives and empower like minds. With the current climate, which is increasingly focusing on empowering those who have long been oppressed, it seems very timely that witchcraft is growing in popularity today.

Living ethically and being environmentally minded - another movement which is becoming more widespread - is also at the heart of modern white witchcraft: witches have an appreciation and understanding of nature and the need to preserve its beauty in order to draw on its infinite power.

White witchcraft is everywhere in the twenty-first century, from the traditional hedge witches - healers that carry the ancient knowledge of the herbal apothecarist - to the celebrity witch vlogger - who will cast you a love spell with likes on your Instagram feed – and everything in between.

Many millennials (although not to rule out older people too!) are turning to witchcraft as their spiritual path, not just for love and prosperity spells but also for self-care, to aid relaxation, and for a more joyful and playful existence. Some of the modern holistic self-care treatments, such as mindfulness, transcendental meditation and affirmations, are great tools for witchcraft, as they teach you to focus on the here and now, as well as instilling the ability to block out peripheral "noise", cultivate self-awareness and reach mentally for your goals. Casting a spell is, above all, the ability to focus your mind on something in order to manifest it.

If your interest has been piqued, there is a list of useful websites and further reading at the end of this book.

BELIEVE IN YOUR INFINITE POTENTIAL. YOUR ONLY LIMITATIONS ARE THOSE YOU SET UPON YOURSELF.

ROY T. BENNETT

GENERATION HEX

"Generation Hex" is the zeitgeist term for all digital-based witchcraft that has mushroomed over the past few years. Young people are increasingly turning to internet-based covens and witchcraft-based social media accounts for support in their daily lives – from confidence charms for their exams to literary essays and podcasts with a witch-based theme to guide them through the myriad social situations and awkwardness of being the first generation to grow up with smartphones and social media.

The internet has also become a powerful tool for unifying like-minded witches and for casting spells, enabling white witchcraft on a scale not seen before. For example, shortly after the surprise inauguration of Donald Trump as US president in February 2017, there was a call to arms among the global witchcraft community via Twitter to perform magic against him, to "bind" him. Binding means to weaken a person's powers for corruption and to protect those in his care from his words and actions. Thousands of witches regularly perform the binding at each waning moon.

There is also a movement called Peace Fires (peacefires.org), which aims to unite people around the world through a healing flame. Anyone can take part in this: you're invited to simply light a candle for an hour or more every full moon from 5 p.m. GMT and state the following intention: "*Let there be peace on Earth and love for one another.*"

ETHICAL WITCHCRAFT

Witches can appear good or dark, and some identify as both, choosing to perform spells both good and bad in their intentions. Those who perform white witchcraft, however, believe in the karmic law and that the craft should only be used for the greater good and never negative purposes. The intentions you send out are returned threefold, which means the bad luck you cast would be three times worse if it found its way back to you.

Be careful what you wish for...

Be sure of the outcome you wish to achieve from a spell before you cast it, and be as accurate as possible when expressing what it is that you desire. If a spell can be misinterpreted, it most likely will be and the result may be far removed from what you hoped for.

OPTIONAL TOOLS FOR WHITE WITCHCRAFT

The most important tool for performing witchcraft is your mind, but sometimes it can be helpful (and fun!) to use a few items to increase the potency of a spell. These are the classic tools in a witch's armoury.

ALTAR

An altar is a safe place to focus your thoughts and energies on performing spells and rituals. It's also the place where you keep all of your tools, such as your wand and book of shadows (see page 18), but it needn't be big – a mantelpiece or bedside table is adequate. The four points of the altar represent the four elements – earth, air, fire and water – and items from nature representing these elements should feature on it. Think of your altar as being divided into quarters which pertain to the following:

North – represents earth. Items that you can place here to represent earth energies include leaves, twigs, stones, salt and crystals.

East – represents air. Items to be placed here include feathers, petals and an oil burner or heatproof dish for burning incense.

South – represents fire. Here place items such as ash, brick, pottery, a small cauldron for burning herbs or paper wishes, and a wand.

West – represents water. This is the place for collected rainwater in a bowl, seashells, driftwood and magic stones (stones with a naturally created hole in the middle).

The centre of the altar should contain your candle or candles for spell-casting.

It's important that you make this space personal to you, so choose items that resonate with you. Keep a white candle on the altar and light it occasionally to purify the space. Your book of shadows must be kept in a safe place – like a diary, it's a personal record and it's not for prying eyes.

MAKE YOUR OWN 'PORTABLE' ALTAR

If you are out and about and want to perform a spell in nature, you can make your own portable altar. It must be made with something that can form an unbroken circle or square and, again, use an item that resonates with you. It could be a piece of twine that you have found on a beach walk, with the ends tied together so that the twine can be stretched into a circle when placed on the ground, or perhaps you have a silver chain that you always wear, or you can simply draw a shape with chalk. Look out for natural altars – it could be a tree stump or a round piece of driftwood. As soon as you've trained your eye to look, you will soon find many possibilities with found objects. Not only is it free, but eco-friendly and sustainable too!

You might wonder why the magic needs to be "contained" in a circle or square. It is this sacred space that ensures protection from negative forces when spell-casting, and concentrates the magic in one place. The circle is believed to symbolize the womb and feminine power, whereas the square altar represents the four elements (one for each corner). The shape of your altar is up to you, but the magical elements must be contained within it when performing a spell.

WAND

Wands are often used as a tool for practical magic by the modern-day witch. They are a way of directing the magic into a particular place and building up energy during a spell. You don't need to spend money on a wand – a twig will suit, but you can't just snap it off the nearest tree; you must ask for the blessings of the woods before you take it. Never use green wood, as this is likely to crack. Green wood contains sap – you want a twig that has been dried out. The best wood is that which has fallen from the tree and been left to dry on the ground. Hazel is traditionally used for wands as it symbolizes fairness, equality and wisdom. Other woods you can use include driftwood that has been smoothed by the waves and still contains the energy of the sea.

You can personalize your wand by painting or drawing witchcraft symbols onto it (see page 96), or if a crystal or found object has a particular resonance for you, such as a piece of sea glass or perhaps a scrap of fabric from a much-loved item, you can add it to the tip of the wand.

BOOK OF SHADOWS

This is the place where a witch records their rituals and spells, like a witchy recipe book. It's helpful to keep a record of when you performed a spell, the ingredients used, perhaps how you were feeling at the time, the moon's phase and the outcome. It means you can look back on your spells and see what has worked and what hasn't, and perhaps consider ways of tweaking them if you were to perform them again. The term "book of shadows" was coined by Gerald Gardner, the founder of modern Wicca, as he recommended that the book be kept hidden – in the shadows – and private. The traditions of witches and their practices have been kept alive by these books.

Your own book of shadows can be as basic or elaborate as you wish – a simple notebook will suffice, but it can be personalized in all manner of ways, such as scenting the pages with your favourite oils, or perhaps decorating the cover with images from magazines or the internet that speak to you in magical ways. Many twenty-first-century witches choose to document their practices on a computer – but make sure you back it up! You could have a special USB stick to store your book of shadows and create a special pouch for it out of fabric.

CAULDRON

Traditionally, this is a large cast-iron vessel with a large mouth. When placed on or beside an altar, the cauldron represents earth because it has a practical purpose, though it symbolizes all of the elements when in use. Cauldrons are still used today in white witchcraft for mixing herbs, burning incense and for performing wish spells – a spell in which powerful hopes are written on paper and burnt in a cauldron so that the thoughts enter the ether in curls of smoke.

Other objects that are sometimes used include:

- **Athame** – a type of knife used to inscribe words and symbols onto candles (see candle spell on page 94).

- **Bells** – these are sometimes rung in banishment spells.

- **Chalice or vessel for water** – this can be used in spells where water is an important component, such as scrying (fortune telling).

A spell to remove a curse

Bells have long been used for cleansing bad energies or removing a hex or curse. First you must prepare the bell for spell-casting (see page 31). Stand with your feet hip-width apart, with hands crossed at the stomach, and the bell in your dominant hand. Then raise your hands over your head, keeping them crossed, before dropping them down again to the starting position, allowing the bell to chime. Do this three times while visualizing the negativity dispersing and dissolving to nothing.

CANDLES

Candles are not essential but a flame is a powerful conductor for your intentions. Different colours of candle wax are traditionally used for different types of spell, for example:

- **Blue** – protection from evil spirits, healing

- **Gold** – wealth and success

- **Green** – money, luck, curing illness, growth

- **Red** – luck, love and romance, prosperity and healing

- **Silver** – fertility, success

- **White** – new beginnings, creativity, purification

Again, if you use a candle for a spell and perhaps the colour doesn't feel right to you, swap it for one that does.

INCENSE

As with candles, burning incense creates an ambience to help focus your mind when spell-casting. Particular aromas are associated with different beneficial properties and can help empower the spell you are casting:

- **Acacia** – for clairvoyance

- **Angelica** – for protection

- **Basil** – for money and fertility

- **Bay** – for lifting a curse

- **Catnip** – for love, happiness, friendship and courage

- **Cedar** – to heal a fraught mind

- **Camomile** – for a change of luck, circumstance or prosperity

- **Cherry** – for love and friendship

- **Chives** – for banishing negativity

- **Cinnamon** – to attract money

- **Clove** – to stop negative words being said about you

- **Comfrey** – for safe travel and protection

- **Dill** – to protect new life

- **Fern** – to encourage rainfall

- **Frankincense** – for good luck

- **Garlic** – for protection and dispelling negativity

- **Lavender** – for good sleep and to attract new love

- **Mint** – for healing and protection

- **Patchouli** – for fertility

- **Pine** – for exorcism and to return negative vibes to their senders

- **Sage** – to cleanse bad energy and for repulsion spells

- **Thyme** – for good health and healing

- **Vetivert** – for protection against thieves and black magic

- **Willow** – to attract love

- **Wisteria** – for protection

- **Ylang-ylang** – adds potency to love and healing spells

CRYSTALS

All natural forms – including you – vibrate at their own frequency. In humans, these frequencies are fluid and can vary depending on your state of health and well-being. Crystals can be used to alter our frequencies as they are also alive with natural energy. They are also highly conductive – and are used in electrical products because of this – which makes them the ultimate power source when casting spells. Each stone possesses different energies and properties, and they can be used to align our own energies too. Here are some of the most potent:

AGATE

This is a soothing and positive stone that will protect the wearer from danger and helps to make sudden changes less daunting.

AMBER

If you are experiencing a lot of negativity, wear amber to repel these bad energies. Amber is also the problem-solver of crystals, resolving misunderstandings and disagreements.

AMETHYST

Place one of these purple crystals by your bed to aid sleep, particularly if you are feeling anxious.

AQUAMARINE

This ice-blue stone symbolizes hope and good fortune. It's often worn or carried when travelling, as it has protective qualities and helps to prevent mishaps.

CARNELIAN

This fiery orange stone revives and restores. It boosts sensual spells and also helps to cut negative ties that are a drain on your mental and physical well-being.

FLUORITE

Fluorescence was first observed in this stone, hence its name. It is a mineral composed of calcium fluoride and is used to absorb negative energy, encouraging positivity and balance. It has healing properties, particularly for ailments relating to skin and the nervous system.

HAEMATITE

The energy in this shiny grey stone aids those with poor circulation and poor concentration, so it's particularly good for long rituals to keep your mind fresh and alert. It's also used in spells to encourage good luck into your life.

JADE

This lush green stone symbolizes longevity and strength. It's used in spells for the attainment of knowledge, specifically information to resolve a difficult situation or conflict.

LAPIS LAZULI

This deep blue stone pertains to wisdom, intellect and the healing of headaches and sore throats. It also has clairvoyant properties; lapis jewellery is frequently worn by witches to help them harness their psychic abilities.

MOONSTONE

This milky white stone has an affinity with its namesake, the moon. It's linked with femininity, fertility and to the lunar phases. It is used in spells for clairvoyance and fertility.

CLEAR QUARTZ

Clear quartz is abundant and has the most far-reaching properties of all the crystals. It can be a powerful catalyst in wish spells, and it aids the healing of both physical and emotional imbalances, as well as any situation requiring a positive outcome.

ROSE QUARTZ

This pale pink-coloured stone is associated with love. Place rose quartz on windowsills to help love flow in and out of your home and use it for spells to draw love into your life. It's also believed to calm nerves and soothe worries – carry a piece around with you in your pocket when you have a difficult day ahead.

TIGER'S EYE

This stone has vivid gold and brown stripes resembling its namesake. It is used for seeing into the future and to help anticipate major events – good and bad – so that you are forewarned. The stone can also be used to find solutions to upcoming difficulties, and in spells to help find employment.

HOW TO LOOK AFTER
YOUR WITCH'S TOOLKIT

There are a number of ways to cleanse and purify your tools for witchcraft so that old spells and ideas don't "stick" to them.

WATER

Simply cleanse the items in running water and pat dry.

SUNLIGHT OR LIGHT FROM A FULL MOON

Some witches prefer to bathe their objects in the light of a full moon or sunlight to cleanse them, preferably for a full day or night. Before you can use your wand for spells, you must purify and empower it by the light of a full moon. Stand outside with your wand on a full-moon night and point it at the moon to draw down its power.

SALT

This is a preservative, and not just in the physical sense. It is used in spells for purification and to cleanse objects of old magic. The item to be cleansed should be fully submerged into salt for a couple of hours. However, do your research beforehand as salt can discolour some items, such as crystals.

SMUDGING

Light a smudge stick (often made of dried sage or cedar leaves), or something similar, for a smoke cleanse. Only do this if you don't have children or animals in the house, and be considerate of other people present – the smell can be quite potent because this kind of purification involves wafting the smoke around to cleanse the air. The sage in a smudge stick is believed to alter the ionic composition of the air, which actively reduces stress levels and, in turn, feelings of anger or upset. Smudging is ideal for dispersing negative energies around the home or office, or to dispel a bad atmosphere after an argument (see page 84 for how to make a smudge stick and for a smudge stick spell).

MINDFUL CLEANSING

This is when you use the power of the mind to cleanse an object. Focus on the object and imagine a pure white light, like sunlight, enveloping it.

THE POWER OF THE MOON

The moon has always held a powerful spiritual significance for witches. Many cast their spells in accordance with the phases of the moon, as each phase has pertinence to different types of spell. A pocket diary will contain the moon's phases, or you can find this information online.

New moon: new beginnings

This is the perfect time to perform spells that herald new beginnings as the new moon represents positive change. Use the new moon's power for finding employment, new love or a new home. It's also a potent time for fertility spells.

Waxing moon: growth and bloom

This is when the moon is growing each night before becoming a full moon. This period is good for attraction spells – ones to grow your wealth, improve health and draw friends and lovers to your side.

Full moon: full power

This is the most powerful time for magic, so use this period wisely by casting spells for protection, wealth, love and good health. Some witches also experience heightened psychic ability during a full moon.

Waning moon: removal and letting go

This is when the moon appears to recede each night in the sky and it's the ideal time for repulsion spells – for example, if you want to banish negative forces in your life, to take control of a difficult situation or soothe a fractious or anxious loved one.

Dark moon: introspective

This is when the moon appears to be invisible, and this phase occurs three days prior to a new moon. Those who perform dark magic are particularly active at this time, and many white witches choose not to cast spells during this period. However, others see it as a good time for spells for breaking negative cycles and bringing justice to bear.

Lunar eclipse (or blood moon)

A red full moon occurs during a full moon lunar eclipse, when the earth passes between the sun and the moon. Lunar eclipses are slightly less common than solar eclipses – there can be between none and three per year – and they are considered by some to be portents of destruction and doom. But with every ending there is a beginning, so they can also be signs of regeneration and renewal, and spells performed during a blood moon can be for positive purposes too.

Solar eclipse

A solar eclipse takes place when the moon passes between the sun and the earth. Some witches believe that when the sun is blocked, the power can't be harnessed for spell-casting at that time so prefer to wait until the eclipse has passed. Others believe that you can capture the power of the eclipse to boost your spell-casting.

ALIGN WITH NATURE...
MAGIC HAPPENS.

JOHN FRIEND

How to capture the energy of a solar eclipse

Solar eclipses are relatively rare; approximately two to four take place each year, and any given area of a 50-mile (80-km) radius will see only one per century. If you are fortunate enough to live in a place that will be experiencing a solar eclipse, or are able to travel to it, here's a way to harness its power to supercharge your spells.

Make a solution of water (any type is fine – sea, mineral or tap), a pinch of salt (not needed if you're using seawater) and a thimbleful of white wine vinegar. Give the solution a good mix and place it outside during the eclipse to absorb its power. After the eclipse, decant the solution into small bottles, such as vials, to wear around your neck or into a jar to sit on your altar. It can also be used in water spells – see page 67 for more.

A FULL MOON RITUAL TO
PERFORM WITH FRIENDS

Many witches charge up and cleanse their crystals and wands by the light of the full moon. If you are using your wand for the first time, you must always purify and empower it by the light of the full moon (see page 31).

This simple full moon ritual offers a chance to focus on ambitions and new ventures, or, if there is nothing specific that you are aiming for, a boost of positivity, which is always welcome!

This ritual is nice to do with a group of like-minded friends. Find a quiet outdoor space – perhaps a garden so that you are not going to be interrupted or overlooked. Begin by making a circle with string or yarn. It needs to be large enough for the group to sit comfortably around it. Tie the two ends of the circle together to make the thread continuous. Light a tea-light each inside the circle and place in a heatproof container with sides, such as a bowl or a hurricane lamp, so that they aren't easily snuffed out by a gust of wind. Have a small piece of rose quartz beside each person but within the circle. Place short lengths of fabric beside each person round the circle. These could simply be oddments picked up from a haberdashers or a torn-up old T-shirt that's past its best. The person who called the ritual may open the circle with the following words:

> *Here tonight a circle spun*
> *For enchanting spells to be done!*

Then the same person picks up a length of fabric, ties it to the string circle and says what they would like to achieve or manifest before the next full moon. Going clockwise around the circle, the next person picks up a piece of fabric, ties it to the string circle and says something that they would like to happen or experience, and so on. Keep going around the circle until everyone has spoken. If there is nothing in particular that you wish to achieve, then you can give thanks for your blessings. When the hopes, wishes and blessings are all attached to the string, everyone must pick up the circle and say this moon blessing:

Full moon, bright moon, hear my plea,
Blessings come, return to me.

Focus on the flickering candles and feel the full moon's energy. Close the circle by holding hands, blowing out the candles and all saying, "So mote it be." Each person can take their piece of rose quartz and keep it with them until the next full moon when the ritual can be performed again.

SPELL-CASTING AND THE
DAYS OF THE WEEK

Each day pertains to a planet and a colour, and certain spells will have extra resonance when performed on a specific day.

SUNDAY

Represented by the sun and the colour gold, this is the best day for spells pertaining to achieving personal goals – such as finding a job or new revenue streams – and improving self-belief, health and well-being.

MONDAY

Represented by the moon and the colour silver, this day is ideal for spells related to family and healing.

TUESDAY

Represented by Mars and the colour red, this day is for spells of passion, though not necessarily affairs of the heart – it could be a personal goal that you wish to achieve.

WEDNESDAY

Represented by Mercury and the colour yellow, this is a particularly good day for casting money and business spells.

THURSDAY

Represented by Jupiter and the colour blue, this day brings strength to spells associated with partnerships - these could be personal as well as professional. All aspects of learning and gaining wisdom are also strong themes on this day.

FRIDAY

Represented by Venus and the colour pink, this day is for love spells, as well as ones for fertility and creativity.

SATURDAY

Represented by the earth and the colour brown, this is a day for spells that signify endings as well as fresh starts, and for banishing bad habits.

BEFORE YOU CAST A SPELL

Performing a spell requires concentration and clarity –
you're not going to do anything well if you're thinking
about what to cook for dinner or looking round at dusty
surfaces or unopened post. If you're performing magic
at home, cleanse the space. Make it clean and tidy, so
that the natural energies in the house can flow freely.
Open the windows to refresh the air. If you've had a
long day at the office, take a bath and relax, and put on
some comfortable clothing made of natural fabrics that
feel nice against your skin. Begin with a meditation or
mindfulness exercise to help ground yourself and prepare
for focussed thought. Here is a simple meditation to get
you in the mood for magic:

*Stand or sit outside. Bare feet are optional, but can help
you to feel grounded as you sense the energy of the earth
beneath you. Listen to the sounds around you – the
birds in the trees, the buzzing of insects – and notice the
earthy, natural smells. Have your palms open, focus on
your breathing, and allow your stomach to rise and fall.
Imagine you are breathing in the sunlight (or moonlight*

*if it's night time). Visualize each breath flooding your
body with golden light. Feel energized and ready for
casting a spell.*

If an indoor meditation is preferred, find a comfortable
and quiet place to sit, light a candle and focus on the
flame as it dances in front of you. Imagine the golden
light from the candle swirling around you as you breathe
in its energy.

A word on "success" in spell-casting

Successful spell-casting can be defined as manifesting what you desire – whether it's a mood, an item or an experience. Always be realistic: don't ask for a big lottery win as it's highly improbable that you will get it – the universe knows when we're being greedy! Be aware of self-doubt too, as this can linger as we consider the things we really want. We wonder if we deserve those things, whether we are good enough, whether we're ready for the challenge. Manifesting desires requires a deeper sense of self-awareness and self-belief: knowing the direction you wish your life to go, and illuminating the path with the help of white witchcraft. Being honest with yourself is key, or you're likely to manifest something that you don't really want after all.

ELEMENTAL SPELLS AND RITUALS

White witchcraft harnesses the power of the four elements – earth, air, fire and water – for casting powerful spells. Using these elements for spell work – such as channelling the power of stormy weather to quell negative energies, using fire for passion, burying something in the earth for renewal, or floating wishes out to sea – will increase the potency of your magic. The next four sections focus on each element in turn and their positive qualities, and guide you through some simple spells and rituals to perform.

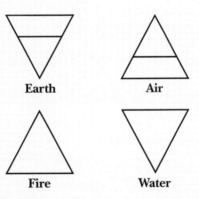

Earth

Air

Fire

Water

WITCHCRAFT IN HISTORY
WAS HUNG,
BUT HISTORY AND I
FIND ALL THE
WITCHCRAFT THAT
WE NEED
AROUND US, EVERY DAY.

EMILY DICKINSON

EARTH SPELLS

An upside-down equilateral triangle
with a horizontal line inside.

Earth spells are used for nurturing and helping things flourish, such as growing or unifying a family, boosting finances, encouraging good health and achieving goals. Simple ways to add earth power to your spells include using soil, living plants or seeds from your garden, salt, crystals (particularly the darker-coloured ones, such as jet), or earthy-smelling incense such as sage and patchouli in smudge sticks.

NEW BEGINNINGS
SEED-PLANTING RITUAL

The new moon is the first stage of the moon's cycle, which means that with every calendar month (every 29.5 days to be exact) the opportunity to start afresh and focus on new goals comes too. Despite the moon not being visible in the sky during the new moon phase, it's considered a fertile time for manifesting – the perfect time to plant seeds of change. This makes sense, as farmers in ancient times used the moon's phases to monitor when to plant and when to harvest, the new moon being the optimum time for planting crops.

Moon phase: within two days either side of the new moon
Day of the week: any

You will need:
- Pen and paper
- Sage plant

This simple ritual is best performed within two days either side of the new moon. It's also a good idea to start thinking about what you wish to manifest a few days before casting the spell, so that when the time comes, you are clear of your intentions.

You can do it anywhere that you feel most relaxed and able to focus. It could be in a quiet spot in the garden, beside your altar, or in your bedroom. On your paper, write down five things that you would like to manifest by the time of the following new moon. Make them positive, like affirmations: short sentences that you can say to yourself each morning for the next month, such as:

- *I feel confident in my decision-making*
- *I have a strong relationship with [...]*
- *I will get a promotion.*

When you have written your list, light a white candle to cleanse the space. Clear your mind and stare intently at the flame flickering, feeling the gentle rise and fall of your chest as you take calm breaths. Think of the universe and your place within it, visualize yourself achieving the items on your list. How does it feel and what does it look like? Then read out your list, saying, "So mote it be" at the end. Spend a good 10 minutes considering your list. Then snuff out the candle and plant your list in the garden under a young sage plant. Water the plant each day, and every time you do so, repeat your list out loud.

So mote it be!

This may seem a mysterious phrase to say at the end of a spell but it is common in Neopagan rituals and modern-day witchcraft. It means "so may it be" or "so it is required", and affirms the intent of the spell, similar to saying "amen" at the end of a prayer.

EVERYWHERE WE LOOK,
THE COMPLEX MAGIC
OF NATURE BLAZES
BEFORE OUR EYES.

VINCENT VAN GOGH

MAKE A SHAMBLE TO GROW
YOUR PERSONAL POWER

A shamble is purported to boost the power of your spell and, in turn, your personal power. "A shamble" sounds like a mess and so it is in a physical sense, but it's essentially about creating order using the chaos of nature. A shamble is not too dissimilar to a dreamcatcher or misshapen spider's web, but it's created from found materials, such as windfall twigs, leaves, feathers, bits of wool that you might find in your pocket – anything that you can weave together. The shape and construction isn't important but one element must be "alive" or from something that is alive, such as a bud or a seed, an eggshell or a dead beetle (one that has passed due to natural causes). Creating your shamble requires a focus that is akin to mindfulness – as you make it you should be fully in the present and aware of your senses and purpose. This mental focus is then woven into your creation, capturing the essence of that moment in time.

Tips for creating a shamble

To maximize its potency, pick a new moon or full moon to create your shamble, or a day that is particularly special to you. Take yourself on a walk in the great outdoors in a place that you enjoy visiting. Search around for items that catch your eye. These could be natural or man-made, but you will need to find some windfall twigs or sturdy grasses to make your frame. Now find a place to rest and begin weaving the elements together. Be as intricate as you like. The focus and care that you take to create your shamble will reflect favourably on your spell-casting. When your shamble is finished, secure the "living" element into the centre of it. Hang it above your altar, or near to the place you choose to perform your rituals and spells.

A RITUAL FOR BURYING BAD ENERGY BETWEEN TWO PEOPLE

Rose quartz is good for healing a love quarrel, whereas fluorite is good if it's more a battle of wills! (See crystals and their properties and how to prepare them for magic on page 26.)

Moon phase: waning
Day of the week: any

You will need:
- A hen's egg
- Two crystals – one for each person involved
- Your wand
- A trowel
- A quiet spot in the garden

Begin by very carefully cracking your egg into a bowl so that you have two eggshell halves that can be pushed back together. Discard the egg's contents (or save it for lunch!). Place the two crystals into the eggshell and push the two halves back together to seal the stones inside – be extra careful when doing this so that the shells do not crack.

Next, go out into the garden with the eggshell. Draw a small circle in the soil with your wand, using an anticlockwise motion, approx. 4 inches (10 cm) in diameter. Then, using your trowel, dig a hole within the circle. Place the egg inside the hole and cover it, patting down the soil. Once this is done, say the following words:

> *Spirit of the Earth*
> *Bring me peace*
> *Awaken hope*
> *Let the discord cease*
> *So mote it be.*

Visualize the earth absorbing the quarrel and the sadness, and in its place positivity and happiness flourishing.

Deosil and widdershins!

Take note of the way you draw your real
or imaginary circles with your wand when
performing a spell or ritual. To attract
something, be it luck, love or good news, circle
the tip of the wand in a clockwise motion (deosil
or sunwise); whereas drawing it anticlockwise
(widdershins) will repel something, such as bad
energies or whatever you wish to banish from
your life.

EARTH MAGIC CAN HELP TO SORT OUT, WORK THROUGH AND SOLVE MANY OF THE MINOR CRISES AND PROBLEMS FACING US AS INDIVIDUALS TODAY.

SCOTT CUNNINGHAM

A TALISMAN TO STAY GROUNDED

This is a simple ritual to help you keep your head in stressful situations. It's best performed on a waxing moon and in a place outdoors where you feel happy, or somewhere that has a positive resonance to you.

- -

Moon phase: waxing moon
Day of the week: any day, but a dry day is best!

You will need:
- A necklace and a glass vial pendant with a secure lid

Begin by casting a circle in a clockwise motion with your wand, with the point of your wand directed at the earth. Make the imaginary circle big enough for you to stand in and step inside it. Feel the power of the earth drawing up through your body. Breathe in the energy and breathe out tension and worry. Imagine your stresses being carried away on the breeze. Do this for several minutes until you feel light with calming energy.

Without moving from your spot, take your necklace, stoop down and fill the small vial with soil from within your circle, using your fingers. Secure the lid of the vial. Leave the circle and say thank you to the earth for its healing energy.

Wear the necklace to give you grounding power whenever you need that extra bit of reassurance in a challenging situation.

Grounding yourself when you feel a sense of unease

A great way to ground yourself when you're in the midst of turmoil is to take some deep breaths and visualize roots growing from your feet and into the ground. Stand firm like a tree while the chaos around you blows through your branches and disappears on the breeze.

MAKE AN ACORN WISH BAG

When autumn is in full flow and the leaves have turned every shade of orange, go out and gather dried windfall acorns on a country walk. Collect these within four days of a full moon, as the moon's power bestowed upon them is said to attract prosperity and good luck for the following month. It can also ward off illness, which is particularly useful during coughs and colds season!

Moon phase: new moon
Day of the week: Sunday, Monday or Tuesday

You will need:
- A small fabric drawstring bag
- A pen and small piece of paper (sticky-note size)

Place a couple of acorns in your drawstring bag. On your paper, write down a wish that you would like to manifest in the coming month. Fold up the paper and pop it into the bag with the acorns.

Carry the wish bag in your pocket or handbag for safe keeping.

Go on a witchy forage

Found objects have a particular potency when spell-casting, so keep your eyes open for natural objects that catch your eye. For example, sometimes the shape and smoothness of a stone can feel nice in your palm, or an autumn leaf in a fiery red sings against the dark earth and makes you want to pick it up, or a feather might float past you on the wind that you manage to catch. When items speak to you in such a way, gather them and save them for spells. However, be sure to thank the earth for its gifts before you take them.

A SPELL TO GROW YOUR CONFIDENCE

This spell will give you a boost when you need it most.

Moon phase: new moon or waxing moon
Day of the week: any time

You will need:
- Fern fronds or leaves, approx. 2 inches (5 cm) in length
- A piece of paper, approx. A5 size
- A piece of garden twine, approx. 10 inches (25 cm) in length
- A green felt tip pen
- A green tea-light candle

Gather your fern fronds at the new moon, as this is a time for positive change and lasting hope. Be sure to thank the plant for the fronds (although you don't need to do this bit out loud!). Cast a temporary altar (see page 17) and place your green candle and fern fronds within it. Light your candle. On your paper, write a simple incantation to call upon nature to help you grow your confidence. It could be something like this:

> *I call upon the energy of the earth*
> *Your strength unfurls*
> *As mine within me*
> *To bring me confidence*
> *So mote it be.*

Make a simple envelope out of the paper and place the fern fronds inside. Next, wrap the twine in a clockwise motion around the envelope and carefully seal the twine by dripping the green wax onto it. Sit for a few moments and absorb the energies of the spell while watching the flickering flame. Then snuff out the candle to complete the spell. Leave the package on your altar until the full moon (or next full moon if you are performing it on that day) and then bury it in the earth – either in the plant pot of a thriving plant or directly into the soil in your garden.

THE SEA, ONCE IT
ITS SPELL, HO
ONE IN ITS NE
WONDER FOR E

JACQUES COUSTEA

WATER SPELLS

*An upside-down equilateral triangle that
symbolizes feminine energy and the moon.*

Water is cleansing, fluid and alive, and is
therefore a potent element for cleansing
bad energy as well as healing spells. It's also
used for water scrying or in divination to aid
clairvoyance. The power of the sea or a flowing
river can heal many ills as well as tempt lovers
to return.

RAINWATER PROTECTION SPELL

This spell for protection will help to allay fears and dispel negative energies, ushering in a renewed sense of calm.

Moon phase: waning moon
Day of the week: any

You will need:
- A candle
- Rainwater that has been collected in a container, such as a jam jar, and empowered by a full moon

First, light your candle in a safe place by the main entry point of your home. (A white candle for cleansing is best, but if you have a particular colour that makes you think of home then use that.) Pick up your rainwater container. Walk around your home and at every entryway to the outside, dip your finger in the rainwater and mark the entry points with a cross. Each time you do this, say the following:

> *With the power of this sacred water*
> *Protect this house*
> *So mote it be.*

When you have placed a cross at every entryway, and returned to the front door, the spell is complete and you may blow out your candle.

MANIFEST YOUR GOALS WITH THE NEW MOON TIDE

The tides are controlled by the gravitational pull of the moon, and this powerful energy source can be used for manifestation. This simple spell is a great way to harness the dual power of the moon and the sea, as well as an opportunity to pause and reflect on your dreams and deepest desires.

Moon phase: new moon
Day of the week: any

You will need:
- Paint or pens
- A coastal beach location
- Wand (optional)

Take a walk along the shoreline of a sandy beach – paddle in the sea, look to the horizon and allow your vision to absorb the vastness of the ocean. Inhale deep breaths of sea air and feel nature's energy course through you. As you walk along the beach, look for a small piece of driftwood to carry. Take note of the silky surface of the wood from years of being tumbled and smoothed by the tides. Find a quiet spot close to where the waves lap, and with your piece of driftwood or wand write a short affirmation in the sand that defines your desire, such as:

- *I want to be confident*
- *I want to find love*
- *I want to feel fulfilled at work.*

Then watch as the waves absorb your words. Take the piece of driftwood home, and with paints or a pen, write the same words that you wrote into the sand onto the wood and keep it on your altar, or in a place where you can see it every day.

PSYCHIC BREW

We would all love to peer into the future, just for a few moments, and this special psychic tea will help to develop your pineal eye (your all-seeing eye) and awaken the psychic abilities that we all possess.

- -

Moon phase: any
Day of the week: any

You will need:
- A pinch of fresh peppermint leaves (or a peppermint teabag)
- A cinnamon stick
- A sprinkling of cloves
- Water
- Honey to sweeten

Place the peppermint leaves, cinnamon stick and cloves in a teapot. Add just-boiled water, stir clockwise to help the elements blend, and steep for a couple of minutes. Strain the tea into a cup and inhale the aroma. Look into the bottom of the cup and recite the following mantra:

My eyes are open
I seek the future
My mind is clear
I'm ready for the truth and have no fear.

Add a teaspoon of honey and take a few sips. Imagine your psychic eye opening and revealing what will soon manifest. Feel each sip awakening your psychic senses.

A WATER SPELL
FOR CLAIRVOYANCE

This spell is akin to the ancient art of reading tea leaves. It requires practice – at first you might think that you can't see any identifiable shapes, but you will soon begin to see motifs forming as the dried mugwort swirls in the water and starts to clump together.

Moon phase: new
Day of the week: any

You will need:
- A candle (white or blue are good colours for this spell)
- A cauldron or container that will hold water
- A piece of silver – this can be something small, like a ring

- Mugwort – preferably dried (this long-leafed aromatic plant is commonly found in hedgerows, or you can purchase it in natural health shops)
- Water

This spell is best performed indoors, unless it's a perfectly still day. Fill your cauldron with water and drop your silver item in. Light your candle and remove other light sources. Sprinkle the mugwort over the water and wait for it to settle. Focus on the surface of the water and think of a burning question that you have, then wait for images to appear to guide you towards an answer. The mugwort will create shapes but witches claim to see images too. This spell is a great way to use your cauldron.

Mugwort and fortune-telling

Mugwort is one of the most magical plants in the witch's apothecary cabinet. It has been used for many purposes over the centuries, from divination and scrying spells and helping you remember your dreams when placed under your pillow to being incorporated in protective spells and charms when gathered in abundance on St John's Eve (23 June) and placed over doorways to stop bad spirits from entering the home.

IF THERE IS MAGIC ON THIS PLANET, IT IS CONTAINED IN WATER.

LOREN EISELEY

BATH MAGIC

Bathing is a ritual in itself. It's an ancient practice for physical and spiritual self-care spanning all cultures. Bathing offers a chance to meditate and reflect on life in peace, but it's also an opportunity to gather energies from nature and attract positive change. To prepare the bath, make sure the room is fresh and inviting; perhaps open the windows, light candles, place crystals beside the bath, gather petals to sprinkle onto the bath and aromatic oils to scent the water. This ritual offers an opportunity to get creative, depending on what it is you wish to attract into your life – use the crystal, incense and plant properties guides in the book to help you choose the right ones for you.

If you wish to attract a lover, for example, have rose quartz beside the bath, red candles, rose petals and jasmine or rose oils. If you wish for calm, allow yourself to be soothed by lavender oils, use white candles and clear quartz. For healing and self-care, use orange blossom and myrtle.

When the bath is ready, enjoy a long soak and inhale the scents while focusing on the goal you wish to manifest. Aim to take a magic bath a few times a week to help build the energy to propel your goals into fruition.

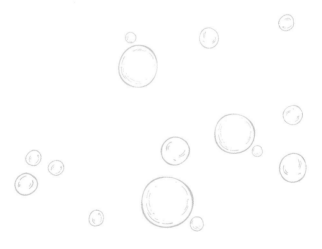

NO MATTER HOW IMPORTANT EVERYTHING ELSE IS TO MAGICAL SUCCESS, BELIEF IS THE MOST CRUCIAL.

DOROTHY MORRISON

FIRE SPELLS

*An equilateral triangle symbolizing masculine
energy and both destruction and creation.*

Burning candles and incense are the most
accessible and safest ways to introduce fire
to a spell. It takes enormous energy to create
fire, and fire spells can be quite tempestuous
and powerful as a result. These spells are for
passion, banishment and big changes.

A FIRE SPELL TO END A RUN OF BAD LUCK

Sometimes it feels like life has dealt you a bad hand – all sorts of problems could be blowing up around you or perhaps you're a little more clumsy than usual and things are breaking or refusing to work. Here's a spell to help get you back on an even keel and rid any bad energies that may be lurking.

- -

Moon phase: waning
Day of the week: any

You will need:
- A piece of paper
- A pen
- A cauldron, or heatproof dish in which paper can be burnt safely

- A small green or white candle (green represents growth and healing, and white represents purity and protection)

Begin by making your home and altar clean and tidy, so that all negative energies and old worries are swept away.

Use the pen and paper to write down a list of all the bad things that have occurred, or negative thoughts that you have been experiencing recently – be as detailed as you can. Light the candle on your altar and focus on the flame, imagining the light from the candle cleansing the space. Take the piece of paper and carefully use the flame from the candle to set it alight, then place the lit paper in your heatproof dish or cauldron until it burns to cinders.

While your bad luck burns to nothing, recite the following:

> *Bad luck from my recent past*
> *Will burn away and never last*
> *Good luck sail forth and return to me*
> *With love and care*
> *So mote it be!*

Once the paper has burned to ash, extinguish your candle with thumb and forefinger or a candle snuffer.

RETURN TO SENDER SPELL

As previously mentioned, performing spells that could cause harm to others is against the white witch's lore, but if you find that you are the subject of a hex or malicious gossip then this spell will deflect the negative energy. Smudge sticks have been used for thousands of years to disperse bad energy. They are fairly simple to make – using fresh herbs bound with string – but they need to be prepared in advance and dried before use. If you don't have a smudge stick to hand, here's a "cheats" version.

Moon phase: waning
Day of the week: any

You will need:
- A piece of parchment paper (approx. A4) that can be made into a small paper bag

- Gummed paper tape, or washi tape
- A handful of dried sage and sagebrush leaves
- A sprinkling of cloves
- Charcoal stick
- Twine
- Matches
- Heatproof dish or cauldron in which items can be burnt safely

Create a small bag out of the parchment paper and secure the edges with paper tape, leaving an opening. Gather dried sage and sagebrush leaves, cloves and a small piece of charcoal stick and place them all into the bag. Tie up the bag with twine and pop it in your heatproof dish or cauldron. Light the smudge stick/bag and walk around the house to allow the incense to permeate all areas. Then open the front door and place the heatproof dish on the doorstep until the smudge stick has burned down to ash – leave it there until the following day. Dispose of the ash around the roots of a fruit tree or potted plant. If you know the name of the person who is gossiping about you, whisper their name as you watch the burning embers.

ATTRACTION SPELL

If only we could charm people into doing what we wanted – life would be so much easier! Although you can't without serious repercussions, this spell is the next best thing. Instead of altering a person's mindset, you're altering the natural, magical energies swirling around you and weaving them into a net to catch opportunities zipping around the ether.

- -

Moon phase: full or waxing moon – it can be performed over five consecutive nights to boost the spell's potency, but always on a waxing moon, or within four days of a full moon.

Day of the week: any

You will need:
- Salt

- Two or three candles – depending on the thing or person that you wish to attract, such as love (red for passion; white for kindness; green for money luck – see candles, page 24)
- A piece of paper
- A pen
- Matches
- Cauldron or heatproof dish in which items can be burnt safely

Find a quiet sanctuary to perform this spell – somewhere you won't be disturbed and you can focus fully on your intentions. Create a safe space by sprinkling a circle of salt around you and your altar. Place the candles close together on the altar and the cauldron beside them. Take the pen and paper and write your intention. For example, if it's to attract a job opportunity, be as detailed as you can about the type of position that you are looking for.

Examine what you have written and really feel those words as you read them. Now light your candles and focus on the dancing flames giving light and energy to your desires. Take the piece of paper and set it alight using each flame, then drop the lit paper in your cauldron and watch it burn, all the while focusing intently on what you want to attract.

MAKE YOUR OWN GODDESS CANDLE

Channel your inner goddess and create your own candle that encapsulates your dreams and wishes. This spell is very much of your own making and design, and it allows you to consider your needs and desires while spending time wandering in your own thoughts and daydreams.

- -

Moon phase and day of the week: any

You will need:
- A simple candle-making kit
- A collection of found or made objects that have potency to you

Make the candle as per the kit's instructions. While the wax is in liquid form, carefully drop your collection of items into it. Use any items of your choosing – for example something whose beauty has drawn you to it, or something that captures the spirit of a place or holds a special memory of a particular moment. These could be things like a dried seedpod or a skeleton leaf picked up on a walk, an acorn to symbolize growth, or a piece of sea glass. Drop your items near the outer edge of the candle so that they are visible once the wax sets. Use whatever smells you love – your signature scent or sprigs of rosemary or lavender (see information on incense and crystals on pages 23 and 26 for inspiration).

The thought and care that you put into the candle will return to you each time you light it, as each element has been carefully chosen by you.

GRATITUDE SPELL

This is a lovely spell that is almost like a self-care exercise – one that invites you to count your blessings, thank the universe, and look back at all the good things happening in your life. Green-coloured items are encouraged for this spell, as this is the colour of heart-felt gratitude.

- -

Moon phase: waning or new
Day of the week: any

You will need:
- An A4 sheet of green paper
- Green pen
- Green tea-light candle
- Green bowl or glass jar

Cut your sheet of green paper into simple leaf shapes, around 3 inches x 1 inch (8 cm x 3 cm) in size. When you have a nice amount of leaves you are ready to perform the blessing. Light your green candle and focus on the flame for a few minutes as you allow positive thoughts of happy times to flood your mind. On each paper leaf, write a few words about something that you are thankful for. When you have finished, pick up each leaf in turn and place it in your bowl or jar and say thank you, either out loud or in your head. Allow the candle to burn out and leave the stub beside the bowl or jar of leaves. The piled-up paper leaves will serve as a constant reminder of how blessed you are. You can add to it when a new blessing comes your way.

A SPELL TO DETER AN EX

We all want to be loved and cherished, but there are times when we just want to be alone, such as after a break-up. This spell will send a firm message to your ex that you want them out of your life and to stop contacting you.

Moon phase: waning
Day of the week: any

You will need:
- A pen
- A piece of paper
- A cauldron or heatproof dish in which paper can be burnt safely
- Matches
- A jam jar two-thirds filled with water

Begin by writing the name of your ex on the paper. Then crumple it and place it in your cauldron or heatproof dish. Light the paper and say the following words:

> *Your love for me has now burnt out*
> *The flame cleanses away your presence*
> *Your presence in my life is no more.*

When the paper has burnt to ash, pour the water from the jar over it and say:

> *Your love is now extinguished*
> *Your presence in my life is no more.*

Swirl up the mixture and pour it back into the jam jar. Screw the lid tightly onto the jar, place it in the freezer and recite these words:

> *Your fire that burned for me is now ice*
> *I shall hear from you no more*
> *So mote it be.*

At the next full moon, take out the jar and defrost its contents before pouring it into the soil outside.

CANDLE SPELLS

There are many types of spell that involve lighting a candle, but one way to make the spell more personal to you is to carve symbols and words into the wax. The way to do this is to gently heat the edge of the candle to soften the wax slightly, and use either an athame (see page 20) or a pin to inscribe details. Many witches use symbols instead of words, but you could start simply by writing your name or the name of the person that you are creating the spell for. Think of symbols that have resonance to you. It could even be a simple rendering of a happy or celebratory emoji to denote a successful outcome to an event or circumstance that is causing you to worry. Here are some symbols that can be used for candle spells but, as with anything to do with magic, it's your mind and your initiative that will boost the potency and eventual outcome of a spell.

AS SOON GO KINDLE FIRE WITH SNOW, AS SEEK TO QUENCH THE FIRE OF LOVE WITH WORDS.

WILLIAM SHAKESPEARE

Symbols for candle spells

Widdershins

Deosil

Yonic

Earth

God

Goddess

Earth

Pentagram

Fire

Air

Water

Pentacle

Protection

Spring

Fall

Protection

Winter

Time

Protect
3 children

Summer

$ Money

Protect
1 child

Protect
2 children

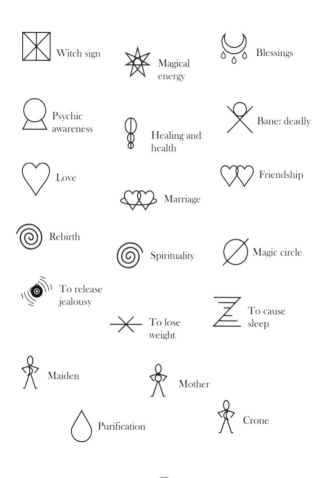

Witch sign

Magical energy

Blessings

Psychic awareness

Healing and health

Bane: deadly

Love

Friendship

Marriage

Rebirth

Spirituality

Magic circle

To release jealousy

To lose weight

To cause sleep

Maiden

Mother

Purification

Crone

PREDICTION CANDLE SPELL

Here's a simple spell if you want a question answered. It requires a beeswax candle and a dark room, so it's best to do this at night at your altar. Light the candle and allow it to burn for a few minutes. Then ask a question and keep a watchful eye on the flame – restrict the questions to ones that only require a "yes" or "no" answer. If the flame starts to bounce and jump, then the answer is "yes". If the flame dips or goes out, then the answer is "no", and if sparks fly, then the outcome will be determined by a force beyond your power. Once finished with your questions, extinguish the flame. Keep this candle purely for prediction spells.

AIR SPELLS

An equilateral triangle with a horizontal line inside.

Air spells are for connecting with others, be it emotionally or spiritually, or to re-establish contact with someone. Air spells also pertain to wisdom and help us to learn more about ourselves, our innermost thoughts and desires.

A FEATHER SPELL FOR
MAKING CONTACT

Found feathers are the ideal item for use in an air spell as they represent communication, flight and pure freedom – the feeling of being untethered, and that anything is possible. If you have a feather in your collection of found objects for magical purposes, try this communication spell if you would like to get in touch with someone from your past.

Moon phase: new or full moon
Day of the week: within four days of full moon

You will need:
• A feather (preferably that of a pigeon as they represent communication – these feathers are in abundance in cities, so this spell is ideal for the city witch!)

- Your mobile phone (or the device you most often use as a form of communication)
- A pen
- A small sticky note
- A selection of herbs, such as dill and sage, ideally picked from your herb garden but bought varieties will suffice
- A white candle
- Matches
- A candle snuffer

This spell is best performed either at your altar, bedside table or beside your desktop computer. It requires total, almost meditative, concentration, so make sure you will not be disturbed. It's best to do the spell before bed, so that you're not using your phone for a while afterwards.

Place your candle on the air quadrant of your altar (see page 15) and light it. Take in some deep breaths, then exhale, as you visualize the peaceful healing light from the candle surrounding you like a protective aura. Place the feather on the altar, also in the air quadrant, along with your communication device. Take the sticky note and write the name of the person that you would like to contact you. Place the sticky note on your device, then take the herbs and scatter them around your phone and the feather and say out loud:

> *Spirits of the air, please ask [insert name here] to contact me*
> *So mote it be.*

Breathe in the energies of the candlelight once more and really focus on the person that you wish to make contact with you – visualize them calling or texting, or writing an email to you, and where they might be at the time. Spend a few minutes in concentrated thought before snuffing out the candle (not blowing it out). Keep the items in place overnight to give the energy of the spell a chance to develop.

A note about free will

White witchcraft will not allow mind control and it is important to remember this, particularly for love spells, where the intention is to attract a particular person. If the union was never meant to happen, chances are it never will.

WILD WEATHER

From the awesome power of a thunderstorm to the crispness of a cold autumn day, the weather is something endlessly fascinating and defines how we live our day-to-day lives. Different weather patterns can also be used to enhance your spells – particularly storms and the direction of the wind.

Heavy rain – perform healing spells in heavy rain, as the rain will help to purify negative thoughts and emotions.

Snowy weather – like heavy rain, snow is good for purification and healing spells. It's also restorative and transformative, and can be channelled for love and friendship spells.

Strong winds – this is good weather for message spells and re-establishing contact with someone.

WIND DIRECTION

North wind – when the north wind blows it can enhance spells that evoke an action or incident from the past, whether it is about healing a rift or coming to terms with loss.

South wind – the south wind gives a boost to spells of confidence and is like a friendly but gentle nudge for you to go for your desires.

East wind – the east wind guides your intuition, so it is helpful when performing spells where you are seeking an answer or resolution of some kind.

West wind – the west wind aids matters of the heart and helps to guide you on the path to love and improved self-worth.

WISHING BUBBLES

This is the perfect spell for harnessing strong winds to manifest simple wishes, and to have some fun along the way – who doesn't love blowing bubbles?

Moon phase: new
Day of the week: any

You will need:
- A cauldron or heatproof dish
- Bubble mixture and wand
- Incense

Begin by burning the incense in your cauldron or heatproof dish. Allow the scent to permeate the air and pass the bottle of bubbles over it a few times. While doing so, concentrate on your wish and the ideal outcome - imagine it in as much detail as you can. Then take your mixture outside to a quiet spot and blow your bubbles. With each breath, imagine you are filling the bubbles with your wish. Watch the bubbles fly off into the sky, full of your intentions. As they pop, the wish is released.

Last word on elemental spells

After trying a few of the elemental spells, you might find that you have an affinity for one element over the others – you could be a water witch, for example. Favouring one element over the others is quite common, and the best thing you can do is to explore it further and work towards creating your own spells based around your chosen element.

SPELL-CASTING WITH MODERN TECHNOLOGY

Anything can be used to cast a spell, and modern witches often forgo the traditional tools of a wand, altar and cauldron, choosing to use digital devices instead. A virtual altar on a computer screen, for example, can be just as effective as a physical one. Consider the unblinking gaze of someone staring at their mobile phone – this level of concentration suits spell-casting very well! This selection of spells offers ways to use a modern environment and technology for manifesting and healing.

WISH BAGS FOR THE OFFICE

This is another discreet way to perform spells in the office. It's also a nice way to perform a spell for another person. Wish bags often contain a few items such as crystals or semi-precious stones (see page 26), or items that are significant to the spell, along with a piece of paper with the intention of the spell clearly written upon it. Office items that you could use include:

 A paperclip - these can be bent into a shape to symbolize what it is you want to manifest or change.

 Erasers - these are good for banishment spells. You could write your intention on an eraser and use it until the intention wears off.

Rubber bands – these can be used for love spells or to diffuse a tense atmosphere.

 **Pencils and pens** – these can be used as makeshift wands, but they must be cleansed in the same way as a traditional wand before being used for a spell (see page 31).

 A piece of silver or gold – this isn't generally found in an office unless you work in jewellery, but you can add a piece of jewellery such as an earring for a protection spell or to increase wealth (handy for when you want to ask for a pay rise or promotion!).

The way to ignite the magic in a wish bag is to light a candle and focus your energies on visualizing the outcome of a spell. Therefore this part is best performed outside on a break or before work.

If the wish bag is for a friend or colleague, give it to them along with a small candle, as they will need to light the candle to manifest the spell. Instruct them to light it when they have a quiet moment, and focus on their wish while holding the bag. The candle can be lit repeatedly over several days until it has burned down. Encourage your friend to keep the wish bag with them on their desk or in a drawer.

STICKY-NOTE MANIFESTATION SPELL

This is surely one of the best low-tech items to be found in an office and also ideal for spell-casting. For a manifestation spell, take a post-it, write what you would like to manifest – be clear and as detailed as possible – and place it on your computer screen as you start up your computer. Concentrate on your wish and the post-it as this happens. The energy required to boot your computer will help to manifest the spell.

A LOVE SPELL TO SECURE A DATE ONLINE

Give your online search for love an extra boost with this spell that combines modern technology with candle magic.

Moon phase: waxing
Day of the week: Friday

You will need:
- A screenshot of the object of your desire on your phone
- A dried bay leaf
- A pen
- A candle
- A cauldron or heatproof dish

First open a window – it's about to get smoky! Place your phone on your altar table with the image of your desired date. Write the name of the person on the bay leaf. Bay leaves are powerful for manifesting desires quickly. Look intently at the image on the phone until your intentions are clear. Light the candle (white or pink is best), watch the flame and take deep, calming breaths while staring at the object of your desire. When you have focus, pick up the bay leaf and light it with the candle before placing it in the heatproof dish. The flame ignites your desire and the message will billow out into the universe along with the smoke. Allow the leaf to burn to cinders and extinguish the candle. When the cinders have cooled, dip your finger into them and draw a circle with your finger on your phone screen. The spell is complete. Leave your phone for a while, preferably overnight, to absorb the spell's power.

MANIFESTATION EMAIL SPELL 1

Email spells are super-discreet and can be used for a quick and easy manifestation spell. Begin by creating a new message on your phone, making sure that you address it to yourself. Think of what it is that you would like to manifest. It could be something like wanting a meeting to go well, or acquiring a new client, or to have a good hair day. Write the message as if you're sure it will manifest, for example: "I will have a fantastic new client on my books by the end of today."

Send the message and leave your email account immediately, as you do not want to open the message that you have just sent yourself. Leave it unread until the spell has worked, then view and delete the message.

MANIFESTATION EMAIL SPELL 2

This spell requires a like-minded friend or colleague. Think of an intention and be as clear and succinct as possible, preferably restricting your spell to one sentence, such as "[name] will receive good news about their job search this week", and then write "So mote it be" underneath. Write the type of spell in the subject line and send it to your friend – perhaps tell them beforehand that you are going to do this. Ask them to open the spell the next day and then send it back to you. When you receive it, leave it until the following day and then open it and send it back to your friend. Do this for a week – alternately sending each other the email every day. Your spell should work within one month.

BLACK MIRROR SCRYING

The black mirror – in that rare moment when your phone or tablet is switched off! – can be employed in the same way as water in a cauldron or a traditional black mirror that some witches use for clairvoyance. Staring into the black mirror is believed to be one of the best ways to awaken your psychic abilities.

Moon phase: new or full
Day of the week: any

You will need:
- A smartphone or tablet
- A soft cloth
- Four tea-light candles

Begin by giving the screen a good clean with a soft cloth, then perform a mindful cleanse, imagining a pure white light encircling it. Place the gadget face up on your altar, or create a makeshift altar to contain the spell (see page 17). Place the candles at each compass point around the screen and light them, then extinguish all other light sources. This spell works best at night.

Meditate and soften your gaze on the black mirror, to allow your clairvoyant abilities to surface, and watch and wait for images to appear – these could be physical images or ones in your mind's eye. Try to fix your gaze in one place. The mirror acts as a portal into your subconscious, bringing hidden visions to the surface. Scrying requires patience and it is a skill that develops over time – many report seeing wispy clouds or loose shapes on the black mirror, while others will experience more lucid thoughts – make sure you write down your experiences to allow time to decipher them.

Spend around 15 minutes on this exercise. Slowly bring your awareness back to your surroundings, visualize a calming white light encircling you. Extinguish the candles and allow the smoke to cleanse the screen.

FURTHER READING AND RESOURCES

The Little Book of Spells offers a glimpse into the world of white witchcraft. There are many avenues to be explored – some use Tarot cards or summon goddesses, while others seek out covens to exchange ideas. Here are some illuminating websites and books to help you discover more about white witchcraft.

Alexander, Skye, *The Modern Witchcraft Spell Book* (Adams Media, 2015)

Basile, Lisa Marie and Sollee, Kristen J., *Light Magic for Dark Times* (Fair Winds Press, 2018)

Carvel, Astrid, *The Little Book of Witchcraft* (Summersdale, 2017)

Chown, Xanna Eve, *The Little Book of Tarot* (Summersdale, 2019)

Cunningham, Scott, *Wicca: A Guide for the Solitary Practitioner* (Llewellyn, 1988)

Illes, Judika, *The Element Encyclopedia of 500 Spells* (Harper Element, 2004)

Nozedar, Adele, *The Element Encyclopedia of Secret Signs and Symbols* (Harper Element, 2009)

Sollee, Kristen J., *Witches, Sluts, Feminists* (ThreeL Media, 2017)

www.thehoodwitch.com
Everyday witchcraft, beginners' guides to everything from crystal healing to Tarot and daily horoscopes.

www.lunalunamagazine.com
Online magazine divided into light and dark – "where readers can feed their good and bad ideas". Contains literary essays and poetry covering subjects related to body positivity, self-care and all aspects of witchcraft.

www.marvelandmoon.com
For all your goddess candle needs.

MAGIC IS NOT A PRACTICE. IT IS A LIVING, BREATHING WEB OF ENERGY THAT, WITH OUR PERMISSION, CAN ENCASE OUR EVERY ACTION.

DOROTHY MORRISON

SPELL INDEX

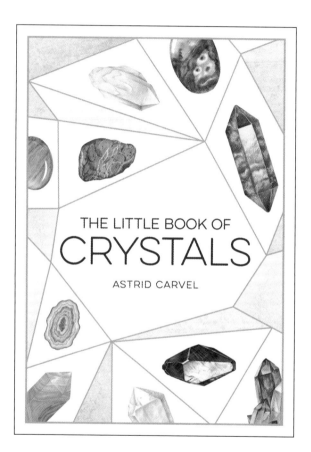

THE LITTLE BOOK OF
CRYSTALS

ASTRID CARVEL

THE LITTLE BOOK OF CRYSTALS

Astrid Carvel

ISBN: 978-1-78685-959-4

Paperback

£6.99

Crystals have long been used for holistic healing purposes. Every crystal emits vibrations, which can help to bring balance, calm and positivity into your life. Learn how to select and maintain your crystals, as well as basic techniques for crystal meditation, balancing chakras and simple ways to bring harmony to mind, body and spirit with these natural treasures. Discover over 50 crystals, their unique properties and how to make use of their power in everyday life, from the love- and harmony-infused rose quartz to memory-boosting amber. There is a crystal for every occasion.

THE LITTLE BOOK OF
TAROT

XANNA EVE CHOWN

THE LITTLE BOOK OF TAROT

Xanna Eve Chown

ISBN: 978-1-78685-798-9

Paperback

£6.99

Have you ever wondered what fate has in store for you?

Since the fifteenth century, Tarot cards have been used as a tool for divination, and a way to shed light on life's questions and challenges. With an introduction to the 78 cards and their symbols, advice on choosing your deck and tips on how to prepare and read your cards, *The Little Book of Tarot* has everything you need to give you your first glimpse into the misty realms of the future... what message will the cards hold for you?

If you're interested in finding out more
about our books, find us on Facebook at
Summersdale Publishers and follow us
on Twitter at **@Summersdale**.

WWW.SUMMERSDALE.COM